From Cupbearer to Leader

God Still Calls Builders

The Blueprint Series

Chris Welch

Copyright © 2026 by Chris Welch and Grit+Grace Leadership

All rights reserved.

No part of this book may be reproduced in any form or by any electronic or mechanical means, including information storage and retrieval systems, without written permission from the author, except for the use of brief quotations in a book review.

 Formatted with Vellum

Dedication

This book is first and foremost dedicated to my Lord and Savior, Jesus Christ. You placed this burden on my heart years ago, and through prayer You taught me to seek revelation, guidance, and divine vision. Then one night in the early morning hours, You woke me from deep sleep, and the Holy Spirit revealed the vision that started it all. Thank You, Lord, for teaching me patience, trust, and the beauty of revelation.

To my wife of over 33 years, Robin, my sweetheart and best friend. I love how you lead with prayer in everything you do and how you encouraged me to keep writing when I wanted to stop. God knew exactly what He was doing when He brought us together in 1989 and joined us in marriage in 1992. You are an amazing wife, an incredible mother, and the best grandmother our family could ever ask for. I can't imagine doing life without you.

To my children, thank you for being my constant encouragement. Watching you thrive and grow in life brings me joy beyond words. Never forget to walk with Jesus; let Him be your guide in all things.

To my grandchildren, Leland and Sage, you make my heart full. I never knew how special being a granddad would feel until you came along. From bike rides to peek-a-boo over FaceTime, every moment with you is a treasure.

To my Life Group and Friday Men's Group, thank you for your love, encouragement, accountability, and unwavering pursuit of Christ. You've challenged me, inspired me, and helped me grow in faith and leadership.

And finally, to you, the reader, thank you for taking time to read this book. My prayer is that through these pages you hear Jesus, find Jesus, and come to know Him personally as your Lord and Savior.

Introduction

When we read the Bible, we can all agree that Jesus was, and still is, the greatest servant leader. But have you ever thought about Nehemiah?

I must admit, I hadn't. If I'm being honest, it had been over 35 years since I had even read the entire book of Nehemiah in the Old Testament.

I knew the Holy Spirit was stirring something in me to write a book. I had tossed around several ideas but couldn't find any peace or clear direction. Then one night in February 2025, I had a hard time falling asleep. Have you ever had one of those nights? Your mind is racing, your thoughts are all over the place, and you just can't seem to get still?

I finally drifted off around 1 a.m., but it didn't last long. The Holy Spirit woke me up. As I opened my eyes, I remember softly saying out loud, "Nehemiah?"

I immediately grabbed my phone from the nightstand and began reading the first chapter of Nehemiah. As I read, I started jotting down what the Lord was speaking to me. Within the next 24 hours, I had a rough outline of a blueprint for leadership, one that Nehemiah lived out through his obedience to God.

Before You Continue

I encourage you to do a few things as you read. First, stop and pray. Ask the Lord to speak to you through the coming chapters and to reveal Himself to you through His Word.

Second, keep a notebook with you. This book isn't meant to be something you just read and set aside. Each chapter will end with reflection questions and a call to action.

Lastly, and maybe most importantly, take what you've learned and use it to add value to those around you. As leadership expert John Maxwell teaches in The 15 Invaluable Laws of Growth, consistent daily improvement is the key to lasting impact.

The Journey from Cupbearer to Leader

Leadership is a journey. Nehemiah's journey began when he started living on the other side of his "yes." He demonstrated powerful lessons in servant leadership. He not only had vision, but he communicated that vision clearly and confidently. And he led with unwavering integrity.

In this book, I want to walk alongside Nehemiah and break down five core leadership principles that we see in his life. These principles, Vision, Courage, Strategic Planning, Perseverance, and Servant Leadership, reveal how Nehemiah's faith, character, and strategy transformed a nation. Through these traits, Nehemiah went from being a cupbearer to a transformational leader.

Vision – Seeing the Need Before Others Do

> *"When I heard these things, I sat down and wept. For some days I mourned and fasted and prayed before the God of heaven."*
> *Nehemiah 1:4 (NIV)*

Vision Begins with a Burden

All great leaders begin their journey the same way, not with a platform or a microphone, but with a burden. Something deep in the heart gets stirred, and a person who might seem ordinary on the outside suddenly finds themselves called into something extraordinary.

That's how it happened for Nehemiah. He wasn't a prophet, a preacher, or a politician. He was a cupbearer, a royal servant in the Persian court whose job was to taste wine before the king did, ensuring it wasn't poisoned. It was a position of trust but not of power. Yet when he heard that the walls of Jerusalem were in ruins and his people were living in disgrace, something inside him broke.

To understand the weight of this moment, you need to

know the context. Jerusalem had been destroyed by the Babylonians nearly 150 years earlier. The temple had been rebuilt under Ezra's leadership, but the city remained defenseless, its walls broken down, its gates burned. This wasn't just about architecture; it was about identity, safety, and the honor of God's people. A city without walls was a city without protection, vulnerable to enemies and ridicule.

Nehemiah's heart moved before his hands did. That moment, when he heard the report from his brother Hanani, was the very moment his leadership journey began. And it all started with one powerful word: Vision.

Scripture says:

> *"When I heard these things, I sat down and wept." (Nehemiah 1:4)*

He allowed the news to reach his heart. He didn't dismiss it. He didn't say, "That's too bad," and go back to business as usual. He wept. He fasted. He prayed. He felt the weight of the need.

Here's what I've learned: Vision begins with a burden, a holy discomfort that refuses to stay silent. It's about being deeply moved by a problem or a need that others might ignore or simply accept. This discomfort isn't a sign of weakness; it's a catalyst for change.

In 2017, I was presented with an opportunity to take over the football radio broadcast for Bushland High School in Bushland, Texas, where we had recently moved. All three of our boys attended school there and played football, so this felt personal to me. But I quickly realized this was more than just a chance to call football games.

I saw something more. I envisioned a broadcasting group that didn't just cover football, but all sports, not just with audio, but with full video production. That spark of vision set in motion what would become Bushland Falcon Media, a full-fledged sports broadcasting network that now covers six sports, has strong community sponsors, and a growing, loyal fan base.

What started with just a phone and a headset wasn't the vision, but it was where the vision was born. This vision continues to grow through the launch of the High Plains Sports Network and through my partnership with godly men at Warrior Garden Studios, who share a vision of creating a space where Christian artists can unite to share the love of Christ through music, podcasts, and other media.

When you live on the other side of yes, when you obey what God calls you to do, He often reveals how your obedience fits into His larger purposes that you didn't even know about. It's not about getting more; it's about understanding more of what He's already doing. I had no idea that saying "yes" to something that seemed so simple, broadcasting sports, was actually preparing me to intersect with other plans He already had in motion.

Vision Requires God's Direction

Nehemiah didn't rush into action. He didn't start drawing up plans or gathering volunteers right away. He spent days in prayer. In fact, the entire first chapter of Nehemiah is his prayer. He confessed his sins, reminded God of His promises, and asked for favor.

There's a leadership lesson here: Before Nehemiah cast a vision to people, he sought direction from God. He was patient. He allowed God to work. We don't always know what He's doing outside of us. As I wrote earlier, He is both Lord and Savior, and by truly understanding that, we have to trust that His plans extend beyond us.

So many leaders want to run ahead of God. I've been guilty of that myself, getting excited about an idea or opportunity and jumping into execution without first spending time in prayer. But Nehemiah teaches us that the strength of our vision is directly tied to the time we spend seeking God.

I've also "sat" on ideas too long. Looking back, I know God moved on because I wasn't acting. And I can say with certainty, I didn't spend that time in prayer asking God for a deeper understanding of His vision. That wasn't patience. It was procrastination.

Don't confuse spending time praying and listening for God to speak with not acting. If you've got a vision building in your heart, pray first. Ask God, "Is this from You?" and "What would You have me do with it?"

If you sit around waiting for God to just speak while you go about your daily activities not in active prayer, that's not a relationship. That's routine. A commander gives orders. A Father gives guidance, and love. He wants to work through you, through your willing spirit. You cannot do that without knowing Him. To know Him means spending time in prayer and reading His Word.

Vision Is Clarified Through Observation

When Nehemiah finally had the opportunity to go to Jerusalem, he still didn't act immediately. He took three days to quietly inspect the damage (Nehemiah 2:11–13). He didn't announce anything. He didn't call a meeting. He got up in the night and walked the city walls to see things for himself.

Why? Because leaders don't speak until they understand. Nehemiah wanted to see what others saw. He needed to know the scope of the work before he could ask anyone to follow.

> Vision moves from idea to clarity when you stop to see what God sees.

This is where vision becomes real. It moves from idea to clarity, from feeling to focus. To be honest, acting on God's vision has never come from instant clarity for me. The focus has always come gradually, like taking steps of faith into what seems uncertain until the ground appears beneath your feet.

That's why preparation matters. If we are in God's Word and in prayer, our eyes are opened. Nehemiah took time to walk around and truly allow God to reveal more to him so that when the time came to speak, he was speaking what God wanted him to speak. He was carrying God's vision, not his own. He understood through God's eyes, not his.

In your own leadership, don't be afraid to step back and observe before you speak. Listen before you lead. See before you build. You want what you're building to stand on God's foundation, not yours.

Vision Inspires Action

Once Nehemiah had clarity, he shared the vision:

> *"Come, let us rebuild the wall of Jerusalem, and we will no longer be in disgrace."*
> *(Nehemiah 2:17)*

Notice the language, "let us." He didn't say, "I'm going to

fix this." He invited others into the vision. True vision doesn't just come from the top down, it's something that ignites others and gives them purpose.

God puts people around you with unique skills and unique purposes. We are not meant to do great things alone. We are meant to do them together. And the people responded:

"Let us start rebuilding." (Nehemiah 2:18)

That's what vision does. It moves people from despair to action, from surviving to rebuilding.

LEADERSHIP CHALLENGE

If God has placed a burden on your heart, don't dismiss it. Don't push it away. Lean into it. Ask questions. Pray about it. Write it down. Go walk the walls, inspect what's broken, what needs healing, what could be rebuilt.

You don't have to be in charge to lead. You just have to care enough to act. Nehemiah was a cupbearer, but he became a leader the moment he let his vision take root.

This week, choose one area of "holy discomfort" and treat it as the starting point of a God-given vision, not just an annoyance or frustration.

REFLECTION QUESTIONS

1. What is something that breaks your heart or stirs your spirit when you see it?

2. Have you taken intentional time this month to pray about the vision God may be placing in your heart?
3. What "walls" around you are broken, at work, in your family, in your community, that need rebuilding?
4. Where might God be asking you to "walk the walls" and get a clearer picture before you speak?
5. Who might God be calling you to lead, not with a title, but with vision?

Call to Action

This week, take time to write out a vision that God may be placing in your heart. Don't worry about perfection, just write what you see, what you feel, and what you hope for. Spend time in prayer over it. Walk the walls, look at what's broken, and ask God how He wants you to respond.

Courage – Leading in the Face of Opposition

> *"I answered them by saying, 'The God of heaven will give us success. We his servants will start rebuilding...'"*
> Nehemiah 2:20 (NIV)

Leadership sounds inspiring, until it costs you something. Vision gets the journey started, but courage is what keeps it moving forward, especially when you face resistance. And if you're doing anything that matters, resistance will come.

Nehemiah faced opposition before he ever laid a brick. The moment he arrived in Jerusalem and made his intentions clear, the critics came out of the shadows. Sanballat the Horonite, Tobiah the Ammonite official, and Geshem the Arab began mocking and questioning him, trying to create doubt and fear. These weren't random critics, they were regional officials who saw a rebuilt Jerusalem as a threat to their own power and influence.

But Nehemiah stood firm and responded with bold confidence in God: "The God of heaven will give us success."

Courage Is Not the Absence of Fear

Courage isn't about not feeling fear, it's about moving forward in obedience despite it. Nehemiah wasn't a warrior. He wasn't born into influence or trained for battle. He was a cupbearer, a servant in a foreign king's court. Yet when God placed a vision in his heart, he didn't let fear silence his calling.

It's a common misconception that courageous leaders are fearless. The truth is, they often feel the most fear, but they've learned that faith is not the absence of fear; it's the decision to move anyway.

Nehemiah had every reason to be afraid. He risked his position by speaking to the king. He faced threats from enemies who wanted him dead. He led a weary, divided people through constant pressure and uncertainty. And yet, he kept building.

Fear whispered, "You're not qualified." Faith answered, "God called me anyway."

Fear said, "The threats are too great." Faith replied, "The mission is greater."

Nehemiah's courage didn't come from personality or position, it came from presence. He stayed close to God. He prayed constantly. He listened before he acted. That's what gave him the strength to face opposition without losing direction.

> Courage doesn't wait for certainty, it acts on conviction.

The Criticism Always Comes

In leadership, if you're building something that matters, someone will always try to tear it down. It's not if criticism comes, it's when.

In Nehemiah 4, as the wall began to take shape, the opposition got louder. Sanballat mocked them publicly, saying, "What are those feeble Jews doing?" Tobiah joined in, ridiculing their efforts: "Even if a fox climbed on that wall, it would fall down!"

Their goal wasn't just to insult, it was to intimidate, to make Nehemiah doubt himself, and to slow the work through distraction. But Nehemiah didn't take the bait. He didn't call a meeting to defend himself. He didn't trade insults or launch a counterattack. He responded with prayer and focus.

> *"Hear us, our God, for we are despised... So we rebuilt the wall till all of it reached half its height, for the people worked with all their heart." (Nehemiah 4:4, 6)*

That's the posture of a wise leader: focused faith over defensive reaction. Nehemiah knew what many leaders forget, criticism is often confirmation you're moving in the right direction.

The moment you start creating momentum, someone will question your motives. The moment you step out in obedience, someone will tell you you're unqualified. And the moment you start building something new, someone will tell you it can't be done.

Expect it. Criticism is part of the cost of calling. People will doubt your intentions. They'll question your abilities. Some may even work against you simply because your progress exposes their passivity.

But like Nehemiah, don't get sidetracked by debate. Don't get defensive. Let the results speak louder than your responses. He didn't waste energy proving himself, he invested it in completing the work.

Nehemiah's response was both simple and profound: He prayed, he planned, and he kept building. His confidence didn't come from approval, it came from purpose.

A Personal Story of Courage in Leadership

When I began leading at a new company, I had a vision to create a weekly space where team members could share what they were working on, speak publicly, and grow their leadership. I saw this as more than just information sharing, I saw it as culture-building.

When I proposed the idea, I hit immediate resistance:
- "We can't do it weekly."
- "No one has time."
- "No one will participate."
- "That's not our culture."

But I couldn't shake the conviction. So I moved forward anyway.

We launched the sessions at lunch, just like I envisioned. Fast forward two years, we had hosted over 100 speakers, our attendance grew steadily, and we built something lasting. What started as resistance became one of the most valued parts of our culture. People who said "no one will participate" became our most engaged speakers.

> That's what courage looks like in leadership: acting when others doubt, and moving forward when God says go.

Courage Strengthens Others

Fear spreads fast, but so does courage. When uncertainty hits a team, a family, or an organization, people look for someone to steady them. They don't need someone who has all the answers, they need someone who has faith.

Nehemiah understood that. In Nehemiah 4, the people were tired, surrounded by enemies, and overwhelmed by the size of the work. The threat was real, and so was their fear. But Nehemiah didn't ignore it or dismiss it, he addressed it head-on.

He stood before the people and reminded them who they were, and more importantly, whose they were.

> *"Don't be afraid of them. Remember the Lord, who is great and awesome, and fight for your families, your sons and your daughters, your wives and your homes." (Nehemiah 4:14)*

That's what courageous leadership looks like. It doesn't minimize fear, it confronts it with faith. It doesn't deny the difficulty, it redefines it through purpose.

When a leader stands firm, it gives others permission to do the same. Your composure becomes their confidence. Your faith becomes their fuel. Nehemiah's courage didn't just move bricks, it moved hearts.

Nehemiah's words reminded his people what mattered most. Their courage wasn't rooted in comfort, it was anchored in remembrance: "Remember the Lord, who is great and awesome." That's what a leader's voice sounds like, it rallies people and reminds them why they started.

Your steadiness can become someone else's strength. When fear spreads, faith must speak, and your voice might be the one that keeps the mission moving forward.

Leadership Challenge

Courage doesn't show up in theory, it shows up in moments. This week, identify one place where fear, criticism, or uncertainty has made you hesitate.

Name it. Bring it before God. Then choose one specific act of obedience you will take, not when it feels safer, but now. Lead the way by moving forward even if your knees are still shaking.

Reflection Questions

1. Where have you allowed fear, criticism, or the opinions of others to slow down or silence your obedience?
2. Whose voice has been louder than God's in your decision-making lately?
3. Think of a time you backed down from something you believed God was asking you to do. What held you back, and what would courageous faith have looked like instead?
4. Who around you needs to see your steady courage so they can find their footing?

Call to Action

This week, identify one area where fear or resistance is holding you back. Write it down. Pray over it. Then take one bold step forward.

And remember Nehemiah's words:

> *"I am doing a great work, and I cannot come down." (Nehemiah 6:3)*

Strategic Planning – Organizing for Success

> *"So I stationed some of the people behind the lowest points of the wall... I posted them by families, with their swords, spears and bows."*
> *Nehemiah 4:13 (NIV)*

Vision and courage will get you started, but without a plan, your leadership can quickly stall. Nehemiah paired faith with structure, and it changed everything.

Strategic planning is the bridge between aspiration and achievement. It's not enough to have a great idea and the bravery to pursue it, you need a roadmap. A well-thought-out plan breaks down overwhelming goals into manageable steps, assigns responsibilities, and provides a framework for tracking progress.

A Leader Who Plans

In Nehemiah 3, we see a brilliant example of strategic leadership in motion. Nehemiah didn't just rally people to build a wall, he designed a system. He took a massive, overwhelming vision and broke it into smaller, manageable assignments.

He divided the wall into sections and assigned each family to build near their homes. That single, intentional decision ensured everyone had clarity of purpose, a sense of unity, and personal ownership of the work.

Each person could see progress right outside their door. Every brick they laid protected their own families, their neighbors, and their future. It wasn't just about rebuilding walls, it was about rebuilding identity and restoring dignity.

Nehemiah understood that motivation grows when ownership is personal. He didn't lead from a distance; he organized up close. He took time to understand the people, their strengths, their fears, and their neighborhoods. Then he positioned them where they could succeed.

He didn't try to do it all. He didn't micromanage or control every detail. He trusted others, and empowered them to lead.

> Great leaders don't do everything themselves, they make sure everything gets done through others.

That's more than delegation; it's development. When Nehemiah handed responsibility to others, he wasn't stepping back, he was pulling others forward.

Each team had a role. Each section had a leader. Each leader had freedom to act within the vision. That's what turns a crowd into a coordinated movement.

Nehemiah's plan was simple but deeply intentional. It created structure without suffocation, alignment without arrogance, and unity without uniformity. Structure doesn't limit passion, it channels it.

That's why planning matters. It's what separates reactive leadership from redemptive leadership. It's the difference between chaos and coordination, between trying harder and leading smarter.

Nehemiah shows us that good management is not the opposite of faith, it's an expression of it. Planning doesn't replace dependence on God; it reflects trust in God's order and wisdom. Nehemiah didn't just pray and hope for a miracle. He prayed, and then he planned.

Planning Starts with Assessment

Here's something I've learned the hard way: you can't plan what you don't understand. Before Nehemiah ever assigned a single person to the wall, he spent three days walking around Jerusalem in the middle of the night, inspecting the damage (Nehemiah 2:12-15).

Think about that. He had the king's blessing. He had the resources. He had the authority to start immediately. But he didn't. He took time to assess the situation first.

Why? Because good planning requires accurate information. Nehemiah needed to know:

- How bad was the damage really?
- What materials would they need?
- Where were the weakest points?
- What challenges would they face?

He couldn't get that information from a distance or through second-hand reports. He had to see it for himself.

I made this mistake early in my leadership. When I first started with Bushland Falcon Media, I thought I knew exactly what the community wanted. I had watched other high school broadcasts. I had ideas. I was ready to go.

But I didn't take time to assess. I didn't ask questions like:

- What do parents actually want to see?
- What technology do our volunteers already know how to use?
- What time constraints do people have?
- What's already working that we shouldn't mess with?

So I jumped in with a plan that looked great on paper but didn't match reality. We had equipment people didn't know how to operate. We scheduled broadcasts at times families couldn't watch. We created content that impressed me but didn't serve our audience.

It took about two months before I realized, I was building MY vision, not the right vision.

So I stopped. I spent time actually talking to parents, coaches, and students. I observed what people responded to. I asked questions. And then, only then, did I rebuild the plan.

The second time around, it worked. Why? Because I assessed before I acted.

That's what Nehemiah did. He walked the walls. He saw what needed to be done. And only then did he call everyone together and say, "Here's the plan."

Planning Requires Communication

Once Nehemiah had assessed the situation, he didn't just start issuing orders. He gathered the people and communicated the plan clearly.

Look at how he did it in Nehemiah 2:17-18:

> *"Then I said to them, 'You see the trouble we are in: Jerusalem lies in ruins, and its gates have been burned with fire. Come, let us rebuild the wall of Jerusalem, and we will no longer be in disgrace.' I also told them about the gracious hand of my God on me and what the king had said to me. They replied, 'Let us start rebuilding.'"*

Notice what Nehemiah included in his communication:

- The current reality - "You see the trouble we are in"
- The vision - "Let us rebuild the wall"
- The why - "We will no longer be in disgrace"
- The resources - "The gracious hand of my God... and what the king had said"

He didn't just tell them WHAT to do. He told them WHY it mattered, HOW it was possible, and WHO was with them. That's strategic communication. And it's one of the most overlooked parts of planning.

I've seen leaders create brilliant plans that fail because they never properly communicated them. They assumed people would just "get it." They thought the vision was so obvious that explanation wasn't necessary. But people can't execute a plan they don't understand. And they won't commit to a plan they don't believe in.

When I was leading that weekly knowledge-sharing initiative I mentioned earlier, the plan wasn't complicated. But I spent significant time communicating it. I met with leaders one-on-one. I explained the why behind it. I painted a picture of what success would look like. I answered questions. I addressed concerns.

And when people pushed back with "that's not our culture," I didn't just say, "Trust me." I said, "You're right, it's not our culture yet. But here's the culture we're trying to build, and here's why it matters."

That's the difference between a plan that dies in a meeting and a plan that actually gets implemented.

> Communication breathes life into strategy.

Strategic Planning turns God-sized vision into tangible reality.

Faith fuels the journey, but strategy provides the roadmap. Nehemiah understood this. He didn't just pray and wait for walls to miraculously appear—he organized his people, allocated resources wisely, and created a plan that empowered every builder to contribute meaningfully.

If you want to lead like Nehemiah, you need to bridge the gap between divine vision and physical completion. That requires intentional structure. It means moving from inspiration to implementation.

The three principles that follow will show you how to transform a scattered group into a unified force and turn a massive, overwhelming goal into achievable reality.

1. Segmentation – Break big goals into smaller, focused efforts.

Nehemiah faced a massive task, rebuilding an entire city wall that had been in ruins for decades. Instead of overwhelming everyone with the big picture, he broke it down into manageable sections. Each group could see visible progress, which built momentum and morale.

Here's what's brilliant about this: when you're staring at a destroyed wall that stretches around an entire city, it's paralyzing. Where do you even start? How do you measure success? When will you know you're making progress?

But when you break it into sections, when you can say, "This family is responsible for the section from the Sheep Gate to the Tower of the Hundred", suddenly it becomes doable. You wake up each morning knowing exactly what you're working on. You can see your progress. You can celebrate when YOUR section is done, even while others are still working. That's the power of segmentation.

I use this principle all the time in leadership. When I'm looking at a big project, let's say we're launching a new broadcast season covering six different sports, I don't look at it as one giant undertaking. I break it down:

- Phase 1: Equipment and setup (August)
- Phase 2: Recruiting and training volunteers (August-September)
- Phase 3: Football season (September-November)
- Phase 4: Basketball and other winter sports (November-February)
- Phase 5: Spring sports (March-May)

Each phase has clear deliverables. Each phase has a team. Each phase can be celebrated when it's complete.

Think about a leader overseeing a church that is growing. Instead of casting one massive, vague vision the Senior Pastor will divide the work into clear teams:

- Hospitality team: First impressions and guest follow-up
- Kids ministry: Nursery through elementary programs
- Worship team: Music and technical production
- Small groups: Connection and discipleship
- Outreach: Community engagement and service
- Facilities: Maintenance, updates and growth focused.

Each team has a leader. Each team knows their win. Each team can measure progress.When people can see progress in their section of the wall, motivation stays high and the vision stays alive.

2. Delegation – Empower others instead of hoarding control.

Nehemiah didn't micromanage or try to lay every brick himself. He identified capable people and trusted them to lead. He gave guidance, not control. That's what healthy leadership looks like, creating space for others to rise.

But here's what I've learned about delegation: it's not just about offloading work. It's about developing people.

When I first started in leadership, I thought delegation meant: "I'm too busy to do this, so you do it." That's not delegation, that's dumping. Real delegation is: "I believe you can do this, and I'm going to empower you to succeed." There's a big difference between those two things.

Let me tell you about a guy named Marcus who worked

on my team years ago. Marcus was talented but quiet. He didn't volunteer for leadership roles. He didn't push himself forward. But I saw something in him.

So instead of just assigning him tasks, I started delegating with development in mind:

- First, I gave him a small project and told him, "You own this. I'm here if you need me."
- Then I gave him a bigger project with more visibility and said, "I trust your judgment. Make the call."
- Finally, I put him in front of senior leadership to present his work and said, "This is your moment. Show them what you've built."

Each time, I was delegating more than just work, I was delegating authority, decision-making, and opportunity. And you know what happened? Marcus grew into one of the strongest leaders on our team. Not because I told him what to do, but because I trusted him to figure it out.

That's what Nehemiah did. He didn't say, "Build the wall exactly the way I would build it." He said, "This is your section. Build it well."

A project manager who insists on approving every decision becomes the bottleneck. But a wise leader sets the direction, equips the right people, and steps back to let them lead. Delegation doesn't weaken leadership, it multiplies it.

And here's the hard truth: if you can't delegate, you can't scale. Your leadership will only ever be as big as your personal capacity. But when you develop others and delegate well, your impact multiplies exponentially.

3. Personal Investment – When people feel personally connected, they take ownership.

Nehemiah positioned families to build near their own homes. When you're building the wall that protects your children, your excellence increases. You care more deeply because the outcome impacts you directly.

This is leadership gold! Nehemiah could have randomly assigned people to different sections. He could have said, "You go work over there, and you work over here." But he didn't. He was intentional about placement. Why? Because when the work is personal, the effort is exceptional.

Think about it: if I asked you to paint a fence for someone you don't know, you might do an okay job. But if I asked you to paint the fence around your own home, the one your kids play behind, the one your neighbors see every day, you're going to do it with excellence. You're going to care about the details. You're going to make sure it's done right. That's not manipulation, that's human nature. And wise leaders leverage it.

When employees or volunteers see how their work connects to something that matters to them, they give more of themselves. Whether it's a volunteer rebuilding a playground in their own neighborhood or a developer improving a product they personally use, ownership changes everything.

As a leader, your job is to help people see the personal connection. Don't just assign tasks, connect the work to what they care about. When people understand how their contribution impacts something they value, their level of commitment transforms completely.

When Plans Meet Reality

Here's something Nehemiah teaches us that a lot of leadership books miss: even the best plans have to adapt.

In Nehemiah 4, everything changed. The opposition got real. Threats were made. The people were afraid. And Nehemiah had to adjust his strategy mid-build.

Look at how he responded:

> *"Therefore I stationed some of the people behind the lowest points of the wall at the exposed places, posting them by families, with their swords, spears and bows." (Nehemiah 4:13)*

He didn't panic. He didn't abandon the plan. He adapted it.

Now half the people worked while half stood guard. Those who were building kept their swords at their sides. They had a trumpet system set up so that if danger came, everyone would know immediately.

The plan evolved, but the mission didn't change. They were still building the wall, they just had to build it differently now.

This is so important for leaders to understand: flexibility is not the same as instability. Adjusting your methods doesn't mean you're abandoning your mission.

Build Your Rally System

But here's what I want you to see, and this is where Nehemiah's leadership becomes absolutely brilliant: He didn't wait for the crisis to figure out how to respond. He built his communication system before he needed it.

Look at what he established in Nehemiah 4:19-20:

> *"Then I said to the nobles, the officials and the rest of the people, 'The work is extensive and spread out, and we are widely separated from each other along the wall. Wherever you hear the sound of the trumpet, join us there. Our God will fight for us!'"*

Think about what this required. The workers were scattered across the entire wall, separated, vulnerable, exposed. If an attack came at one point, how would anyone else know? How would they coordinate a defense?

Nehemiah created a rally system. One signal. One response. Everyone knew what to do. When you hear the trumpet, drop everything and run to that sound. Don't wait. Don't wonder. Don't check your section first. Rally to the point of attack. We'll face it together.

This wasn't reactive leadership, this was strategic preparation. He planned for the crisis before it happened.

> Good leaders respond to crisis. Great leaders prepare for crisis before it comes.

And here's what makes this so powerful: The trumpet system did more than just provide a way to respond to attacks. It created unity. It built trust. Every person working on that wall knew that if trouble came to their section, they wouldn't face it alone. Help was coming. All they had to do was sound the alarm.

That's the power of a good rally system, it transforms isolated individuals into a coordinated force.

What This Looks Like in Modern Leadership

I've learned this lesson the hard way. Early in my leadership, I was great at launching initiatives but terrible at planning for what could go wrong. I'd get everyone excited, we'd start building, and then when crisis hit, and it always does, we'd scramble.

No clear communication plan. No designated response team. No rally point. Just chaos and everyone trying to figure it out on the fly. Now? I build my trumpet systems first.

When we started Bushland Falcon Media, I didn't just plan for successful broadcasts. I planned for what happens when:

- Equipment fails mid-game
- Weather shuts down the event
- Key volunteers don't show up
- Technical issues arise

We created clear protocols:

- Who do you call?
- What's the backup plan?
- How do we communicate with our audience?
- Where do we rally if we need to problem-solve quickly?

It's not exciting. It's not glamorous. But when the crisis comes, and trust me, in live broadcasting, crises come often, everyone knows exactly what to do.

That's what the trumpet system does. It removes panic and replaces it with process.

Three Elements of an Effective Rally System

If you want to lead strategically, you need to build your own version of Nehemiah's trumpet. Here's what that requires:

1. A Clear Signal

The trumpet wasn't subtle. It was loud, unmistakable, impossible to ignore. Everyone knew what it meant.

Your team needs the same clarity. What's your "trumpet"? How do people know when to stop what they're doing and rally?

In some organizations, it's a specific phrase or code word. In others, it's an emergency text or call system. In families, it might be a family meeting that everyone knows means "this is serious."

The point is: don't make people guess. When crisis hits, confusion kills momentum.

2. A Designated Response

Nehemiah didn't say, "When you hear the trumpet, figure out what to do." He said, "Run to the sound. We'll fight together."

Everyone knew the response. No debate. No committee meeting. Just immediate, coordinated action.

What's your team's designated response when things go wrong? Do they know, or do they have to ask?

3. Trust That Others Will Show Up

Here's the beautiful part: The trumpet system only worked if people trusted that help was coming. If you sound the alarm and nobody comes, the system fails.

Nehemiah built that trust by organizing people in families and positioning them to protect what mattered most to them. They weren't just protecting the wall, they were protecting each other.

As a leader, you build this kind of trust through consistency. When someone on your team sounds the alarm, do you show up? Do you rally the troops? Or do you let them handle it alone?

Because if you want people to rally when you need them, you'd better be ready to rally when they need you.

Don't Wait for the Crisis

The biggest mistake leaders make is waiting until they're in the middle of a crisis to figure out how to handle it.

By the time you're under attack, it's too late to create a communication system. It's too late to assign roles. It's too late to build trust.

Nehemiah didn't wait. He saw the threat, assessed the vulnerability, and built the system while they were still building the wall. That's strategic leadership.

So here's my question for you: What's your trumpet system?

- If your team faces a crisis this week, do they know how to respond?
- Have you identified your rally points?

- Does everyone know their role when things go sideways?
- Have you built the trust that makes people willing to drop everything and help?

If you don't have answers to those questions, you're not ready for the crisis that's coming. And trust me, it's coming.

The good news? You still have time to build your trumpet system. Don't wait until you hear the attack. Build it now, while you're building everything else.

Because when the pressure comes, your team won't rise to the occasion, they'll fall to the level of their preparation.

Make Sure They're Prepared

I learned this lesson during the COVID-19 pandemic. We had just gotten Bushland Falcon Media running smoothly with audio broadcasts. We had sponsors, we had equipment, we had processes in place. And then suddenly, everything changed.

But here's what happened: the Texas governing body over high school sports, the University Interscholastic League (UIL), made a decision that opened up a new opportunity. They allowed us to start using video to show sports, which was previously not allowed.

Remember the vision I talked about in Chapter 1? The one where I saw more than just audio broadcasts, I envisioned a broadcasting group that covered all sports with full video production? Well, this was the realization of that vision God gave me.

Most people would have seen that moment as pure chaos. And it could have been. But because we had laid a solid foundation and had technology that was capable of doing more than we needed, we were able to shift quickly.

We already had the equipment. We already had the technology in place. We just needed to make some adjustments, find a camera operator, work on on-screen graphics, figure out the live-streaming logistics.

And suddenly, we weren't just broadcasting audio anymore. We were live-streaming video. Parents, grandparents, and friends who couldn't attend games in person could now watch their kids play. In a time when families were separated and isolated, we became a connection point.

Here's what I want you to see: the adaptation wasn't just about surviving a crisis. It was about being prepared when opportunity met adversity.

God had planted that vision years earlier. I didn't know when or how it would happen, but when the door opened, we were ready to walk through it.

We didn't have to scramble to buy equipment. We didn't have to learn technology from scratch. We didn't have to build relationships with schools and sponsors overnight. All of that groundwork had already been done.

We didn't gain wealth or fame from this pivot, but we did gain the privilege of serving families during a difficult season. That's the real blessing of faithful preparation.

That's what good planning looks like in the real world. It's not rigid. It's resilient. And it's ready.

Nehemiah had positioned people, organized teams, and established communication systems before the threats came. So when opposition showed up, he didn't have to start from zero, he had a foundation to build on.

When the pandemic opened that door for us, we were ready to walk through it. Not because we predicted a global pandemic, but because we had built something solid enough to handle unexpected change.

That's the power of strategic planning. When you plan well, you're not just preparing for the future you can see, you're preparing for the future you can't predict.

Structure Brings Strength Under Pressure

When threats rose, Nehemiah reorganized. The builders worked with tools in one hand and weapons in the other. His plan adapted. His people adjusted. His focus never wavered. That's what strong leadership looks like under pressure.

Strategy isn't rigid, it's responsive. Plans are living documents, not stone tablets. Good leaders don't just build, they prepare.

Nehemiah understood that structure doesn't make you inflexible; it makes you resilient. Because when the pressure comes, and it always does, a healthy structure doesn't collapse; it bends and absorbs the impact.

When enemies threatened, Nehemiah didn't panic or abandon the mission. He assessed, realigned, and redeployed. The workers were repositioned. Guards were stationed. Trumpets were assigned for communication. Every person knew their role and why it mattered. That's organizational clarity under stress.

Nehemiah's situation changed rapidly, and his plan evolved to meet those changes. He adjusted tactics, but never the goal. He didn't lose focus trying to control every outcome. He led through change by keeping his people centered on the mission, not the moment.

Too many leaders cling to their original plans even when circumstances shift, and they end up defending the plan instead of delivering the purpose. Others abandon structure entirely when things get hard, and they drift into chaos and burnout. Nehemiah modeled the balance. He stayed steady, but not stubborn.

The real strength of a leader isn't proven when everything's calm, it's revealed when everything's shifting. When the pressure rises, your structure will either crack or carry you. And if it's built on prayer, clarity, and purpose, it will hold.

A Personal Story of Strategic Planning

Years ago, I was leading a youth group at a small church. We had seen amazing growth over several years. But I grew complacent. One summer, I looked around, and only five students were left.

I went home, prayed, and asked God what happened. The answer was clear: I had stopped leading with strategy. I had drifted from purpose.

The next week, I gathered those five students and read Matthew 28:19: "Go and make disciples…"

I asked, "What does this mean for us?" One of them answered, "We need to go."

That became our plan. We weren't waiting for students to come to us anymore, we went to them. But here's the thing, I didn't just say "go reach people" and hope for the best. We got strategic about it.

We sat down and created a simple plan:

- **WHO**: Each of the five students identified 3-5 specific friends they wanted to reach
- **WHAT**: We planned events that would be

appealing and non-threatening (game nights, movie nights, pizza parties)
- **WHEN**: We scheduled something every two weeks to maintain momentum
- **WHERE**: We rotated between different homes so it felt personal, not institutional
- **HOW**: Each of our five core students was responsible for personally inviting and following up with their list

I didn't ask those five students to just "invite people to youth group." I asked them something more personal. I said, "Who in your life needs Jesus? Who sits alone at lunch? Who's going through a hard time? Who would benefit from having friends who care about them?"

Suddenly it wasn't about growing a program. It was about reaching THEIR friends. It was personal.

One of those students had a friend whose parents were going through a divorce. She didn't invite her friend to youth group because I told her to, she invited her because she genuinely cared and wanted her friend to find peace and hope. That's the difference personal investment makes.

Then we added one more element, incentives. Not as bribes, but as celebrations of progress. I challenged them: "If we reach 20 students, we'll have an ice cream party. If we reach 30, I'll grill steaks."

Two months later, we had fired up the grill and thrown a party. We went from 5 students to over 30. Why? Because we had a plan. God's plan. And it was personal. Each of those five students took ownership of reaching their friends. They didn't just invite people to church, they built relationships with intention.

But here's what I learned: the plan worked not because it was complicated or clever. It worked because it was scripture based, prayed over, clear and it was personal. Everyone knew their part.

That's strategic planning at its best.

THE DANGER OF PLANNING WITHOUT PRAYER

Before we move on, I need to say something important: planning without prayer is just human effort. And human effort alone will never accomplish God-sized dreams.

Nehemiah prayed before he planned. He sought God's direction before he drew up the strategy. And throughout the entire building process, he continued to pray.

When opposition came, he prayed:

> *"Hear us, our God, for we are despised"*
> *(Nehemiah 4:4).*

When he had to make decisions, he prayed:

> *But I prayed to our God and posted a guard"*
> *(Nehemiah 4:9).*

When enemies tried to intimidate him, he prayed:

> *"Now strengthen my hands" (Nehemiah 6:9).*

Prayer wasn't separate from his planning, it was integrated into it. He didn't pray OR plan. He prayed AND planned.

I've fallen into this trap before. I've gotten so excited about a strategy that I jumped straight into execution without stopping to ask God, "Is this what You want? Is this how You want it done? Is this the right timing?"

And you know what happens when I do that? Even the best plans fall flat. Why? Because they're MY plans, not God's plans.

Here's what I've learned:

> The best strategic plan in the world is worthless if God isn't in it.

So before you segment the work, delegate the tasks, and create personal investment, pray. Ask God to guide your planning. Invite Him into the process. Let Him shape not just your vision, but your strategy for achieving it.

Because at the end of the day, it's not about having the smartest plan. It's about having a God-directed plan.

Nehemiah knew this. That's why he could lead with confidence even when everything seemed impossible. His confidence wasn't in his planning abilities, it was in the God who directed his plans.

Staying Focused on the Great Work

In Nehemiah 6, when the wall was nearly complete, Nehemiah's enemies made one final attempt to pull him off course. They sent message after message, inviting him to meetings, trying to create fear, spreading rumors, all with one goal: to distract him from finishing the work.

But Nehemiah's response was firm and focused:

> *"I am doing a great work, and I cannot come down." (Nehemiah 6:3)*

He refused to be sidetracked by noise, fear, or flattery. He knew the difference between what was urgent and what was important.

Let me pause here and clarify something important: when Nehemiah says "a great work," he's not being arrogant or self-important. He's describing his calling, the specific assignment God had given him in that season. Your "great work" is simply your God-given calling at this time in your life. It's the thing God has specifically asked you to do right now.

For Nehemiah, that calling was rebuilding the wall. For you, it might be leading a team, raising your children, serving in ministry, starting a business, or caring for aging parents. The work is "great" not because of its size or visibility, but because God called you to it.

Focus is strategic. Staying on mission is planning in motion. Nehemiah understood something every great leader eventually learns: distraction is the enemy of progress.

When you're building something that matters, opposition will always find a way to whisper, "Come down." Sometimes it shows up as criticism. Sometimes it's comparison. Other times, it's the temptation to chase something easier, faster, or more comfortable.

Here's what distractions look like in real leadership:

- The "urgent" meeting that could have been an email
- The side project that sounds exciting but isn't aligned with your mission
- The criticism that demands you stop building to defend yourself

- The opportunity that's good but not God-directed
- The busyness that makes you feel productive but doesn't move you forward

Distractions are constant. You will be pulled in many directions. That's why strategy isn't just about what you'll do, it's also about what you'll ignore. A strong strategy defines what not to pursue, what meetings not to take, and what voices not to entertain. It protects your focus so your time and energy stay centered on what matters most.

I have to fight this battle constantly. There are always new opportunities, new ideas, new projects that sound exciting. And some of them are genuinely good things. But good things can become distractions from the great work, the calling, God has placed on your life in this season.

That's why I regularly come back to this question: "What is my great work right now? What has God specifically called me to do?" And then I ruthlessly protect time and energy for that calling.

For Nehemiah, the great work was rebuilding the wall. Everything else, no matter how it was dressed up, was a distraction.

What's your great work? What is God calling you to do in this season? And what do you need to say no to so you can stay focused on it?

Leadership Challenge

Take one key area of your life or leadership, a project, a ministry, a team, or even your family, and treat it like Nehemiah's wall.

This week:

- Define the "sections" (segmentation).
- Decide what you will no longer personally control (delegation).
- Clarify who is personally impacted and how (ownership).

Then write one simple, Nehemiah-style sentence that captures your focus. Fill in the blank with your God-given calling for this season:

"I am doing a great work (_____), and I cannot come down."

Reflection Questions

1. Are you leading with structure, or mostly reacting on the fly to whatever feels urgent?
2. Where do you need more planning in the vision God has given you?
3. Who needs to be empowered to lead in your organization, ministry, or home, but is currently waiting on you to let go?
4. What is your "great work", your calling, in this season?
5. What specific distractions (even good things) are trying to pull you down from that calling?

Call to Action

This week, evaluate your leadership strategy.

- Are you organized?
- Is your team clear on the mission?
- What distractions need to be cut?

Write or refine a simple plan for your great work, with clear next steps and clear owners. And if you're tempted to come down from the wall, remember why you started.

Perseverance – Finishing the Work Despite Challenges

*"So the wall was completed... in fifty-two days...
because they realized this work had been
done with the help of our God."*
Nehemiah 6:15–16 (NIV)

STARTING IS EASY. Finishing is leadership. Nehemiah and his team didn't quit, even when they were exhausted, discouraged, or under attack. They built through opposition, through conflict, and through fatigue. That's perseverance.

Perseverance Is Grit + Grace

In Nehemiah 4:10, the people said,

"The strength of the laborers is giving out."

Sound familiar? Every leader eventually hits that moment, the halfway point. The adrenaline is gone, the progress is slower, and fatigue starts whispering, "Maybe this isn't worth it."

That's where Nehemiah stepped in. He didn't shame them for being tired, he reminded them of why they started. He refocused their eyes on the mission and the God who called them to it.

> *"Remember the Lord, who is great and awesome." (Nehemiah 4:14)*

That's what perseverance looks like. It's grit, the resolve to keep going when the excitement fades. And it's grace, the humility to depend on God for strength when your own runs out. Perseverance isn't just pushing through the pain, it's building with purpose while the pressure is on.

Grit without grace becomes striving, not thriving. Grace without grit becomes passivity. True perseverance is the balance between the two, working with determination while trusting with surrender. I summarize it this way:

Built on Grit, defined by Grace.

Nehemiah didn't let discouragement define the moment. He prayed, he planned, and he positioned his people with both swords and trowels. They built and defended at the same time. That's what perseverance does, it doesn't retreat when pressure rises; it adapts and presses forward.

Leadership often requires this dual posture, hands that work and hearts that trust. You keep showing up, not because it's easy, but because the mission is worth it and the One who called you is faithful.

INTERNAL CHALLENGES ARE THE HARDEST

The next challenge Nehemiah faced wasn't from the outside, it came from within. In Nehemiah 5, the people began exploiting one another through debt and unfair practices. The community that had once worked shoulder to shoulder was now divided by greed and injustice.

Nehemiah could have ignored it. He could have said, "Let's just finish the wall and deal with this later." But he didn't. He stopped the work long enough to confront the issue. He held the nobles accountable and called the people back to integrity.

> *"What you are doing is not right. Shouldn't you walk in the fear of our God?" (Nehemiah 5:9)*

That's courageous perseverance. It's easy to stay committed when everyone's united and morale is high. It's much harder when the challenge comes from inside your own camp, when trust erodes, motives are questioned, or personal agendas start to rise.

Every leader will face moments when internal conflict threatens to undo the progress being made. It's in those moments that perseverance takes on a new form, not just endurance, but moral courage.

Nehemiah's strength wasn't only in building walls; it was in protecting the heart of the people behind them. He didn't just want a completed project, he wanted a restored community.

True leadership doesn't avoid hard conversations. It leans into them with conviction and compassion. That's what

Nehemiah modeled, a leader who refused to compromise integrity for the sake of convenience.

A Personal Story of Persevering Through Challenge

You may remember from Chapter 2 when I shared about launching a weekly knowledge-sharing initiative for our staff. About 18 months in, it was gaining real momentum. People were growing. The culture was shifting. Then internal resistance came. Some leaders wanted to repurpose the time, to change the meeting entirely.

I paused, prayed, and remembered why we started. I told my team, "If they want to start something new, we will support that. But we're not replacing what God has clearly blessed."

We were halfway through what most leadership experts say is a 3–5 year culture shift. We weren't about to stop. And we didn't. We stayed the course. The results continue to grow.

Sometimes, perseverance is just showing up and holding the line. Don't stop when you're tired. Stop when you're finished.

Celebrating Progress Without Losing Focus

In Nehemiah 8, the wall was finished. The enemies were silenced. The people had accomplished what once seemed impossible. But Nehemiah knew the mission wasn't over, it was just entering a new phase.

He gathered the people, not to boast about what they had built, but to renew their commitment to the One who made it possible. Ezra opened the Book of the Law, and as the people listened, they wept, worshiped, and remembered. It was more than a celebration, it was a recommitment.

> *"They read from the Book of the Law of God, making it clear and giving the meaning so that the people understood what was being read." (Nehemiah 8:8)*

Nehemiah didn't stop at success. He led the people to sustain it. Because great leaders understand: finishing a project isn't the same as fulfilling a purpose.

True leadership doesn't end at completion, it shifts into continuation. It's one thing to reach a milestone; it's another to maintain what was built and keep growing from it. Many leaders lose focus after the win. The applause fades, the adrenaline dips, and complacency quietly moves in.

But Nehemiah didn't let the people settle. He redirected their attention from the work of their hands back to the condition of their hearts. He knew that walls without worship are just barriers. So he led a moment of renewal, a time to give thanks, to remember God's faithfulness, and to re-center the community on their greater purpose. That's what leaders do.

- They don't just build, they sustain.
- They don't just celebrate results, they cultivate long-term transformation.

Perseverance isn't only about pushing through difficulty; it's about remaining faithful after the victory. It's the daily choice to protect, nurture, and grow the fruit of your effort long after the initial excitement has faded.

Leadership Challenge

Look at one area of your life or leadership where you are "mid-wall", no longer at the exciting beginning, but not yet at the finish.

Name the fatigue. Name the resistance. Then choose one concrete way you will:

- Re-center on why you started, and
- Re-align with Who called you.

Perseverance is rarely flashy. This week, practice it quietly and consistently.

Reflection Questions

1. Where have you been tempted to quit, spiritually, relationally, or in your leadership?
2. Are you mid-build with something God asked you to start? What would "finishing the wall" actually look like?
3. What is testing your endurance right now, external pressure, internal conflict, or simple exhaustion?
4. How do you typically respond after a "win", do you drift into comfort, or lean into deeper dependence on God?
5. What form does perseverance need to take for you in this season: staying, confronting, resting, or restarting?

Call to Action

Write down why you started. Recommit. Refocus. Identify one practical step you will take this week to move the work forward, however small.

And remember: the wall was finished in fifty-two days, because they didn't stop.

Servant Leadership – Leading with Integrity and Humility

> *"But the earlier governors, those preceding me, placed a heavy burden on the people... Their assistants also lorded it over the people. But out of reverence for God I did not act like that."*
> Nehemiah 5:15 (NIV)

LEADERSHIP ISN'T ABOUT TITLES, perks, or power, it's about responsibility, sacrifice, and service. Nehemiah had the authority to lead as governor. He had the political power and the backing of the king. But instead of using it for personal gain, he used his position to lift others up. That's servant leadership.

It's the kind of leadership modeled by Jesus Himself, the King who washed feet. The Savior who said:

> *"Whoever wants to become great among you must be your servant."*, Matthew 20:26

Nehemiah lived this out. And it changed everything.

Choosing a Different Way

In Nehemiah 5, we read that former governors used their position to tax the people heavily and demand special treatment. Nehemiah could have done the same, but he didn't.

He refused to eat the food allotted to governors. He refused to demand money or land. He refused to take advantage of the authority that came with his title.

Instead, he worked alongside the people, not above them. He carried the same burdens they carried. He faced the same dust, fatigue, and pressure they did. He didn't issue orders from a comfortable distance, he led shoulder to shoulder, brick by brick. Why? "Out of reverence for God."

That one phrase defines the heart of a servant leader. Nehemiah wasn't trying to be impressive, he was trying to be faithful. He understood that leadership is stewardship. It's not about position; it's about posture.

He didn't see leadership as a reward to be enjoyed, but as a responsibility to be carried. He understood that true authority doesn't come from demanding respect, it comes from demonstrating integrity.

Servant leaders choose a different way. They lead with open hands, not clenched fists. They use their influence to lift others, not elevate themselves. They measure success not by how much they gain, but by how much they give.

That's what separates self-serving leadership from godly leadership. One seeks privilege, the other seeks purpose. One consumes, the other contributes. One builds a name, the other builds people.

Servant Leadership in Action

Nehemiah didn't just talk about humility, he demonstrated it. He didn't just lead with words, he led with sacrifice. He not only refused to take from the people, he gave to them. He personally funded meals for 150 Jews and officials at his own table. He used his resources to relieve burdens, not create them.

That's what servant leadership looks like, leading with open hands instead of closed fists. He could have lived comfortably. He could have justified the perks. He could have said, "I've earned this." But instead, he said, "God has trusted me with this."

And that shift, from ownership to stewardship, is the foundation of lasting influence.

Servant leaders understand that generosity is not weakness. It's not just kindness, it's leadership in motion. They give because they know what's been given to them. They serve because they understand the weight of being trusted with people, not just projects.

Nehemiah modeled a truth every great leader must embrace: Serving and leading are not opposites, they are inseparable. He didn't see humility as a detour from leadership; he saw it as the path to it.

When leaders act with integrity, humility, and service, trust takes root. And when trust takes root, people follow, not because they have to, but because they want to.

People don't remember how loud you led. They remember how well you loved. When your actions say, "I'm for you," hearts open, unity grows, and teams move with purpose.

A Personal Story of Servant Leadership

Growing up as the son of a pastor, I didn't learn servant leadership from a book, I watched it lived out every day.

My dad pastored a small church, and if something needed to be done, he did it. If no one showed up to clean the church, he cleaned it. If a light bulb was out, no matter how high, he climbed a 16-foot ladder and changed it. He painted, repaired, visited hospitals, counseled families, performed weddings and funerals, many of them for free.

But what stood out most wasn't just what he did, it was how he did it. He treated everyone the same, whether they sat on the front row or the back. He didn't look down on anyone; he lifted them up. He listened, encouraged, and loved people well.

He modeled the kind of leadership that Jesus showed us, leadership that serves before it speaks. And in doing so, he modeled it for me.

Someone once asked me, "Why did you choose servant leadership?" I paused for a moment and said, "It wasn't a choice. It's just who I am."

And the truth is, I couldn't lead any other way. Because once you've seen servant leadership lived out with consistency and grace, you can't go back to positional leadership. You can't unsee humility that leads with heart. You can't unlearn integrity that puts people first.

> You realize that real influence doesn't come from authority, it comes from authenticity.

Taking the Hit for Your Team

Early in my leadership career, I had a moment that tested this deeply. We had just pushed a new application into production, and by Monday morning, everything had gone sideways. Thousands of users, including several Fortune 500 insurance companies, were locked out of their systems. It was chaos.

As a first-line manager, I was in a room with all of my engineers and architects trying to diagnose the issue. Tension was high. That's when I heard my name paged over the intercom, loud and clear. Everyone in the room heard it. I was being called to the CIO's office.

I walked in to find my boss to the right, his boss to the left, and the CIO, former special forces and highly intimidating, dead center. He unleashed a verbal barrage about the failure, the financial impact, and how someone needed to take accountability.

"Someone has to eat this sandwich," he said. (He used stronger language.)

My bosses stood silent.

I leaned forward, put my hands on his desk, and calmly said, "Then feed the sandwich to me so I can get back in the room and fix this."

He paused and replied, "Finally, someone took accountability."

Two things happened that day. First, I served my team. They never knew the full weight of the heat I took on their behalf, but I carried it so they could stay focused on the work ahead.

There were plenty of people I could have blamed. The architect who missed the design flaw. The developer whose code triggered the issue. The tech lead who signed off on the review. The tester who didn't catch the edge case.

But I didn't. Not because I was trying to be a hero, but

because a servant leader takes responsibility before they assign it. It wasn't a calculated decision. It was instinct.

The second thing that happened was something I didn't expect. I earned the respect of my CIO. That wasn't my goal. As I walked down the hall toward my team, my heart was racing. I remember thinking, Well, that might've just been a CLM, a Career Limiting Move.

But as I stepped into the room where my team sat, I felt a strange peace. They looked up, waiting for me to unload or pass down the frustration from above. Instead, I simply said, "It's all good. Let's focus on fixing the issue and getting our customers back up."

They nodded, and we got back to work.

Turns out, it wasn't a CLM after all. In time, that same CIO became a mentor, someone who guided and encouraged me through other tough seasons in my career.

You don't become a servant leader in the big moments. You become one in the small ones, by watching, learning, and choosing humility day after day. Those quiet choices and unseen tests prepare you for the moments that matter most.

The Cost of True Leadership

Servant leadership isn't glamorous. It's not about titles, spotlight moments, or applause. It's about sacrifice, daily, often unseen, sometimes misunderstood sacrifice. True leadership costs something.

It will cost you comfort. It will cost you time. It will cost you the need to always be right. But what it produces is far greater than what it requires.

Servant leadership often means:

- Putting others before yourself, even when it slows you down or goes unnoticed
- Listening when you'd rather talk, because understanding always precedes influence
- Giving credit away and taking responsibility when things go wrong
- Leading without recognition, because you're leading for purpose, not praise

This kind of leadership rarely makes headlines. But it changes lives. It builds trust, the kind of trust that can't be demanded, only earned. It creates loyalty, the kind that lasts when times get hard. And it inspires transformation, not just in outcomes, but in people.

That's why Nehemiah's impact didn't stop with a wall, it reshaped a community. He wasn't just rebuilding bricks and gates; he was rebuilding hearts and purpose. He modeled leadership that was steady, selfless, and surrendered to God's greater plan.

> The greatest leaders don't build monuments to themselves, they build legacies in others.

Leading for God, Not Applause

In Nehemiah 5:19, Nehemiah prays:

> *"Remember me with favor, my God, for all I have done for these people."*

It's a short, quiet prayer, easy to pass over, but it reveals the heart of a true servant leader. Nehemiah wasn't asking for praise. He wasn't keeping score. He was leading for an audience of One.

That's the difference between leaders who serve for recognition and leaders who serve from conviction.

Nehemiah's strength wasn't in his platform, it was in his posture. He led faithfully, not for approval, but out of obedience. And when the work was finished, he didn't demand honor, he simply asked God to remember his heart.

John Bevere is an author of many books I have read. He has challenged me in so many areas of my walk with Christ; but he will be the first to admit that these are not his words, but God's words revealed through the Holy Spirit.

In several of John's books, he reminds us that many people want the stage, but God first tests us in obscurity. True servant leadership always begins in the unseen moments, when no one is clapping, when the work feels thankless, when the results are slow. That's where God measures the heart and shapes a leader who can be trusted with influence.

Nehemiah's story reminds us that lasting impact doesn't come from being noticed, it comes from being faithful.

Public success means little if it isn't rooted in private surrender.

He wasn't chasing fame. He was chasing faithfulness. And that's what God rewards.

When you lead like that, you can rest knowing that even if no one else sees, God does. And that's enough.

> Servant Leadership is not a "someday" calling; it is a "today" responsibility.

Leadership Challenge

As your influence grows, so does the temptation to lead for yourself. This week, intentionally choose one situation where you could use your position for personal benefit, and instead, use it to lift someone else.

Let someone else shine. Take the hit. Give away the credit. Do it quietly, "out of reverence for God," and let that choice shape your heart.

Reflection Questions

1. Do you see leadership as a platform to serve, or to be served? Be honest.
2. How do you handle recognition, status, or power when it comes your way, do you hold it loosely or cling to it?
3. In what specific ways can you practice humility in your current role, at work, at church, or at home?
4. Who in your life has modeled servant leadership well? What habits or attitudes have you seen in them that you need to imitate?
5. Where might God be inviting you into the "secret place" to serve unseen, so He can shape your heart?

CALL TO ACTION

This week, take one intentional action to serve your team or those you lead. Something unexpected. Something sacrificial. Something that reminds people you're not above them, you're beside them.

Lead with humility. Lead with integrity. Lead like Nehemiah.

Living the Blueprint – Your Next 30 Days

"The God of heaven will give us success. We his servants will start rebuilding."
Nehemiah 2:20 (NIV)

You've walked through Nehemiah's story. You've explored the five leadership principles that helped a cupbearer become a transformational leader:

- **Vision** – Seeing the need before others do
- **Courage** – Leading in the face of opposition
- **Strategic Planning** – Organizing for success
- **Perseverance** – Staying faithful when it gets tough
- **Servant Leadership** – Leading with humility and integrity

But what now? How do you move from inspiration to implementation?

This chapter is your guide to live the blueprint. Whether

you're leading a team, a ministry, a business, or your family, these principles are meant to be lived, not just learned.

Step 1: Begin with Prayer and a Burden

Just like Nehemiah, your leadership should start with a burden, a sense of purpose that's bigger than you. Ask yourself:

- What breaks your heart?
- What need do you see that others overlook?

Take it to God. Pray. Listen. Don't rush ahead of Him. Write it down. A burden becomes vision when you begin to name it.

> *"When I heard these things, I sat down and wept... then I prayed before the God of heaven.", Nehemiah 1:4*

Step 2: Clarify the Vision and Cast It Well

People don't follow vague ideas. They follow clear vision. Define your why. What exactly are you hoping to build, restore, or change?

Make it personal. Share stories. Speak from the heart. Invite others in. Use "we" more than "me."

> *"Come, let us rebuild the wall... and we will no longer be in disgrace.", Nehemiah 2:17*

A compelling vision gives people purpose and direction. It turns listeners into builders.

Step 3: Build a Strategic Plan

Vision without a plan is just a dream. Break the work down. Identify phases, milestones, or roles. Position the right people in the right places. Delegate wisely.

Be flexible. Adjust your strategy when needed, but don't change the goal.

> *"Each person worked on the section of the wall nearest their house.", Nehemiah 3*

Good planning aligns your team, multiplies effectiveness, and gives everyone ownership in the outcome.

Step 4: Prepare to Persevere

Resistance will come. Don't be surprised, be ready. Remember why you started. Keep the mission front and center. Watch for internal and external challenges. Lead with integrity through both.

Encourage your people often. When morale drops, your words matter.

> *"Don't be afraid... remember the Lord, who is great and awesome."*, Nehemiah 4:14

Step 5: Stay Grounded in Servant Leadership

Never forget: leadership is a responsibility, not a reward. Stay humble. You're not building your name, you're building something that lasts.

Lead from the front. Be visible, approachable, and present. Protect your people. Own the hard moments, even if no one sees it.

> *"Out of reverence for God I did not act like that."*, Nehemiah 5:15

Great leaders don't just get the job done, they do it with character and care.

Your 30-Day Blueprint Challenge

Here's your challenge: Choose one arena of your life, work, church, community, or home, and intentionally apply all five principles over the next 30 days.

Week 1: Vision & Courage

- Identify your burden and pray over it daily
- Share your vision with at least three people

- Take one courageous action despite fear or criticism

Week 2: Strategic Planning

- Break your vision into 3-5 actionable steps
- Identify who needs to be involved and delegate one responsibility
- Write your "great work" statement: "I am doing _____ and I cannot come down"

Week 3: Perseverance

- When resistance or fatigue hits, revisit why you started
- Address one internal challenge with honesty and grace
- Celebrate small wins with your team

Week 4: Servant Leadership

- Serve someone on your team in an unexpected way
- Take responsibility for something that goes wrong
- Pray Nehemiah's prayer: "Remember me, God, for all I have done for these people"

Don't wait for a title. Don't wait for permission. Start where you are, with what you have.

Reflection Questions

1. Which of the five principles in this book is most natural for you, and which is most difficult? Why?
2. Where in your life do you sense God inviting you to "start rebuilding"? Is it a relationship, a team, a ministry, a habit, or your own heart?
3. What would it look like, practically, for you to lead more like Nehemiah in the next 30 days?
4. Who do you need around you, mentors, peers, or team members, to help you live this blueprint, not just admire it?
5. If someone followed you for a week, what would your leadership tell them about the God you serve?

Call to Action

Take one page in your journal or notebook and write this at the top: "My Nehemiah Blueprint – The Next 30 Days". Underneath the title, list:

- The burden God is stirring in you
- A simple statement of vision
- Three strategic steps you will take
- One way you will practice perseverance when it gets difficult
- One specific way you will practice servant leadership every week

Share this blueprint with a trusted friend, mentor, or

spouse. Ask them to pray with you and check in on your progress. Then start rebuilding.

Conclusion

Leadership isn't a destination, it's a daily decision. Nehemiah's story doesn't end with a finished wall; it continues with a renewed people. That's what true leadership does, it builds something that outlasts the leader.

The steps we've explored through this book, vision, courage, strategic planning, perseverance, and servant leadership, aren't meant to be followed once and checked off a list. They're meant to be revisited, lived, and refined over time.

Every new season will test a different part of your leadership. One day, you'll be called to build. Another day, to fight. And sometimes, simply to stand still and trust. That's the rhythm of leadership, faith and action working together.

> True leadership isn't about building walls, it's about building people.

My hope is that as you close this book, you won't just admire Nehemiah's story, you'll begin to live your own. Because the same God who called Nehemiah to rebuild a broken city is calling you to rebuild what's been broken in your world.

Maybe it's your workplace. Maybe it's your family. Maybe it's your confidence, your purpose, or your faith.

Wherever it is, know this:

God still calls builders.

The Blueprint Series

This book, From Cupbearer to Leader: How to Lead with Vision and Purpose, is the first in a series of Blueprint books designed to guide leaders like you on your journey.

Each volume focuses on a core dimension of leadership, vision, integrity, influence, and legacy, offering biblical principles, practical wisdom, and personal reflection to help you navigate real challenges in real life.

These books aren't meant to be exhaustive reads. They're meant to be companions, something you can pull off the shelf whenever you need a spark of clarity, encouragement, or direction.

When you're wrestling with a hard decision, questioning your calling, or simply needing a reminder that your leadership still matters, open one of these blueprints. They're here to remind you that you're not building alone.

A Personal Word

If there's one message I want you to take from this book, it's this: Seek God first, always. Don't just invite Him into your leadership when things get hard. Include Him in every step, every meeting, every plan, every prayer.

Your relationship with Him isn't a part of your leadership, it is your leadership.

Because when you walk with God, your leadership becomes less about proving yourself and more about reflecting Him. You don't have to be perfect to lead well. You just have to be faithful.

Your brother in Christ, Chris

A Closing Prayer

Father,

Thank You for the example of Nehemiah and for the way You still call ordinary people to do extraordinary things.

I pray for every reader who has walked through these pages, that You would stir their hearts with vision, strengthen them with courage, and surround them with people who share their burden.

Teach them to lead with humility, integrity, and love. Remind them that leadership is not about power, but about service.

May their leadership reflect Your heart in every word and every decision. And when the wall feels too high, the work too heavy, or the critics too loud, help them remember: You are their strength. You are their guide.

In Jesus' name, Amen.

To Download a a group study guide please go to:
http://gpgleadership.com/downloads

About the Author

Chris Welch lives in Bushland, Texas, with his wife Robin of over 33 years. Together they have four married children and two grandchildren (with a third on the way).

Chris serves as a deacon in his local church, leads the volunteer team for media, and leads both a men's group and a life group. He also enjoys broadcasting local sports, riding his bike, and hunting.

Chris wrote From Cupbearer to Leader as a personal response to the prompting of the Holy Spirit and a deep desire to help others grow as Christ-centered, servant-hearted leaders. He believes that anyone, with the right vision, courage, plan, perseverance, and humility, can be used by God to transform the world around them.

Made in the USA
Coppell, TX
28 January 2026

70198666R00046